# MAIL TRAINS

## Julian Stray

SHIRE PUBLICATIONS

Published in Great Britain in 2012 by Shire Publications
Ltd, Midland House, West Way, Botley, Oxford OX2 0PH,
United Kingdom.

44-02 23rd Street, Suite 219, Long Island City, NY 11101,
USA.

E-mail: shire@shirebooks.co.uk    www.shirebooks.co.uk

© 2012 The British Postal Museum & Archive.

A CIP catalogue record for this book is available from the
British Library.

Shire Library no. 657.    ISBN-13: 978 0 74781 083 4

Julian Stray has asserted his right under the Copyright,
Designs and Patents Act, 1988, to be identified as the
author of this book.

Designed by Tony Truscott Designs, Sussex, UK
and typeset in Perpetua and Gill Sans.

Printed in China through Worldprint Ltd.

12  13  14  15  16      10  9  8  7  6  5  4  3  2  1

## COVER IMAGE

*Euston Station: Loading the Travelling Post Office*, 1948.
Artwork by Grace Golden for one of a series of four
posters depicting the work of Post Office staff, for display
near 'working, dining and retiring rooms' in postal and
telegraph buildings.

## TITLE PAGE IMAGE

Fixing the leather pouch holding the mail bags to
the 'traductor'. This would be swung out, leaving the
pouches hanging from the side of the train carriage, to
be snatched by trackside apparatus into a waiting net.

## CONTENTS PAGE IMAGE

The only known surviving complete rail car from the 1863
Pneumatic Railway Despatch Company underground mail
service, discovered underground during road works at
Euston in 1928.

## ACKNOWLEDGEMENTS

Thanks to my colleagues in The British Postal Museum &
Archive for their immense assistance. Particular mention
should be made of Barry Attoe, Martin Devereux, Freya
Folåsen, Vyki Sparkes, Chris Taft and Louise Todd. Special
thanks to Deborah Turton for her patience, support,
proofreading and editing.

The author and images for this book were provided by
The British Postal Museum & Archive.

Apart from those listed below, all images are © Royal Mail
Group Ltd, 2012, courtesy of The British Postal Museum
& Archive, www.postalheritage.org.uk.

Illustrations are acknowledged as follows:

Tony Conder, page 60; Clive Jones, page 24 (top); Bill
Pipe, page 14; Julian Stray, pages 11 (top), 15, 21 (top),
28 (top); 32 (top and middle); Chris Wilson, page 56 (top
and bottom); Stan Withers, pages 59 (bottom) and 61.

## THE BRITISH POSTAL MUSEUM & ARCHIVE

The British Postal Museum & Archive is the leading
resource for British postal heritage. It cares for the visual,
physical and written records of over four hundred years of
postal heritage, including stamps, poster design,
photography, staff records and vehicles. The BPMA is
custodian of two significant collections: the Royal Mail
Archive, and the museum collection of the former
National Postal Museum. The Royal Mail Archive is
designated as being of outstanding national importance.
To find out more, visit www.postalheritage.org.uk

Shire Publications is supporting the Woodland Trust, the UK's leading woodland conservation charity, by funding the dedication of trees.

# CONTENTS

## ANNO PRIMO & SECUNDO

# VICTORIÆ REGINÆ.

✳✳✳✳✳✳✳✳✳✳✳✳✳✳✳✳✳✳✳✳✳✳✳✳✳✳✳✳✳✳✳✳✳✳✳✳✳✳✳✳✳✳✳✳✳✳

## C A P.  XCVIII.

### An Act to provide for the Conveyance of the Mails by Railways.  [14th *August* 1838.]

**W**HEREAS it is expedient that Provision should be made by Law for the Conveyance of the Mails by Railways at a reasonable Rate of Charge to the Public: Be it enacted by the Queen's most Excellent Majesty, by and with the Advice and Consent of the Lords Spiritual and Temporal, and Commons, in this present Parliament assembled, and by the Authority of the same, That in all Cases of Railways already made or in progress or to be hereafter made within the United Kingdom, by which Passengers or Goods shall be conveyed in or upon Carriages drawn or impelled by the Power of Steam, or by any locomotive or stationary Engines, or animal or other Power whatever, it shall be lawful for the Postmaster General, by Notice in Writing under his Hand delivered to the Company of Proprietors of any such Railway, to require that the Mails or Post Letter Bags shall from and after the Day to be named in any such Notice (being not less than Twenty-eight Days from the Delivery thereof) be conveyed and forwarded by such Company on their Railway, either by the ordinary Trains of Carriages, or by special Trains, as Need may be, at such Hours or Times in the Day or Night as the Postmaster General shall direct, together with the Guards appointed and employed by the Postmaster General in charge thereof, and any other Officers of the Post Office; and thereupon the said Company shall, from and after the Day to be named in such Notice, at their own Costs, provide sufficient Carriages and Engines on such Railways for the Conveyance of such

*Postmaster General may require Railway Companies to convey the Mails.*

Mails

# MAIL BY RAIL

WHEN the Liverpool & Manchester Railway opened on 15 September 1830 it affected not only local transport but also the Post Office's arrangements for conveying mail. Locally contracted mail coaches ceased operating in October 1830 because passengers switched allegiance to the railway, leaving the Post Office without transport for the mail. An official was despatched from London to determine the practicality of carrying mail by the new mode of transport and, having no alternative, the Post Office entered a contract with the railway commencing 11 November 1830, enabling mail carriage by train. The following day a Post Office official reported: 'Yesterday I began with the new arrangements on the Rail Way and the Mail Bags were conveyed 4 times with great success.'

By 1836 the Post Office was operating both day and night services on the Liverpool & Manchester Railway, despatched respectively at 14.00 and 17.00, in both directions. Trains covered the 30 miles at a speed of 20 mph. On 28 June 1837 a Post Office surveyor wrote to the Postmaster General:

> ...notwithstanding the great, the important and the extensive acceleration attending the adoption of the railway for the conveyance of the bags, not one town in this district will suffer, all will have the advantage of a quicker return of the answer to the letters despatched to the north.

As mail volumes increased, road mail coaches were too small to handle the quantities to be carried. When an experimental penny post was set up between Stockton-on-Tees and Middlesbrough in January 1833, it was so successful that it continued the following year, generating a profit of £40. The number of letters and papers rose from 7,100 in the first year to 9,675 in the second, so to handle this increase the first public railway in the world, the Stockton & Darlington Railway, was incorporated into the scheme in 1835.

Rail carriage brought speed to the mail operation. In May 1837 Scottish newspapers reported that the time for conveying post between London and Edinburgh would reduce to just four days. Not everyone, however, approved

Opposite:
The Railways (Conveyance of Mails) Act, 1838, granted the Post Office power over the United Kingdom's railways. The Postmaster General could call on any railway company to run a train for mail at times fixed by him. Companies also had to provide and fit out sorting carriages or convey mail by ordinary trains if required.

The Bath–London Mail Coach: an engraving illustrating the precursor to the mail-bag exchange apparatus later used on mail trains; bags of mail are snatched from the hand of the postmaster as the coach passes without stopping.

of the Post Office transferring mail to the railway. In 1837 several manufacturers complained to the Postmaster General that as a consequence of the railway new road services were running through Matlock, Bakewell and Buxton, thereby serving agricultural districts, and bypassing the manufacturing towns of Leek and Macclesfield. Little could be done; the contractor who had previously operated the Derby to Manchester mail coach stated that it was no longer profitable because the railway had taken all passenger traffic. Several mail-coach operators asked to be relieved of Post Office contracts; the comments of the Birmingham to Liverpool operators were typical: 'Since the opening of the Railway, all trade has left the Mail.'

Occasionally mail operations on the railway preceded its opening to passengers. The Grand Junction Railway first conveyed passengers on 4 July 1837, but an evening despatch of London mail had been sent from Birmingham to Liverpool the previous day. The Post Office Superintendent of Mail Coaches, George Louis, travelled with the mail, at first by road to Coventry, and then by railway from Birmingham. On reaching Liverpool, Louis wrote to the Postmaster General:

This is the first time in Europe so long a journey was performed in so short time and if some very few years ago it had been said a letter would be answered by return of Post from London the idea would have been hailed as criminal and yet at 8 last evening was I in London and this letter will reach there tomorrow morning, the proceeding of these operations occupying a period of 34½ hours only out of which a rest of three hours is to be taken thus performing a distance of 412 miles in 31½ hours!

Transported by train, the London mail to Liverpool and Manchester took just fifteen and a half hours.

Beyond the simple carriage of mail, experiments were held with sorting mail whilst in transit on the railway. As early as 1826, Rowland Hill, the man later to be responsible for uniform penny postage, had written about the possibility of sorting letters along the road

in specially fitted mail coaches. In 1837 George Karstadt, a Post Office surveyor, suggested using a special railway carriage for sorting mail whilst en route. The idea was tested on 20 January 1838 between Birmingham and Liverpool on the Grand Junction Railway. Manned by Edward Ellis and Frederick Karstadt, George's son, it consisted of a converted horse-box temporarily fitted out to allow mail to be sorted on board. Following the successful trial, the Grand Junction Railway was instructed to build four such 'railway post offices' specifically for the service. These carriages were fitted with letter-sorting frames and measured 16 feet in length.

This trial was so successful that in June 1838 the Post Office made railway post offices a permanent part of postal organisation, and the Railways (Conveyance of Mails) Act, 1838, was passed by Parliament. This obliged railway companies to provide a separate carriage for sorting letters en route or to convey mail by ordinary trains if needed. For this they were granted

*Last of the Mail Coach Guards*, by H. E. Brown, c. 1890: a portrait of Moses Nobbs in uniform. The longest-serving mail guard in the Post Office, he served fifty-five years (1836–91) on the mail coaches and later on the Post Office railways.

A mail-coach guard's frock coat, manufactured by Herbert & Co, London. When mail was transferred from mail coach to train, mail guards frequently did so too, still wearing their smart scarlet double-breasted uniform.

The working area on board the first bespoke sorting carriage built in 1838 was smaller than shown here. The simple 'pigeonhole' sorting frame, with a well below for unsorted mail, remained a feature of railway post offices for over a century and a half.

'reasonable remuneration', based on awards given by the Railway and Canal Commission, to which was referred any dispute between the Postmaster General and a railway company that could not be resolved by negotiation. Other routes were quickly established, with railway clerks appointed to sort letters on board. The arrangement, tying, sealing, despatch and receipt of mail bags was carried out by mail guards. Carriages were fitted with small chimneys to vent the pots in which wax was melted for use when sealing the necks of mail bags.

Design by Rosalind Dease for a 5d stamp, featuring the 1838 travelling post office on the London & Birmingham Railway, submitted for the 1969 Post Office technology stamp issue but not adopted.

1838 travelling post office

POST-OFFICE

5d

When the first stage of the London & Birmingham Railway opened on 17 September 1838 the Post Office began sending mail by rail directly from London. The first train to include a purpose-built sorting carriage also ran along this route, initially from London Euston to Denbigh Hall, near Bletchley. The problem of carrying mails further was answered by loading mail coaches on to rail trucks at Euston and then offloading them complete with mail at Denbigh Hall. Passengers simply moved from railway carriage to mail coach for the remainder of the journey. The London to Birmingham line soon opened throughout its entire length, and by the end of 1838 the railway had reached Preston.

Mail for Ireland travelled by rail from 24 January 1839 via the London & Birmingham, Grand Junction and Liverpool & Manchester railways, before being transferred to steam packets at Liverpool for the sea crossing. When the Chester & Holyhead Railway opened in May 1848 a faster route became available and what would become known as the 'Irish Mail', the oldest named train in the world, ran for the first time on 1 August 1848 between London Euston and Holyhead.

The Louth–London mail coach leaving Peterborough station on its last journey, on 19 December 1845, carried on the newly opened Peterborough to Blisworth railway. Initially mail guards travelled above and behind mail coaches until complaints about cinders led to them being supplied with 'shades for the eyes', and finally moved inside.

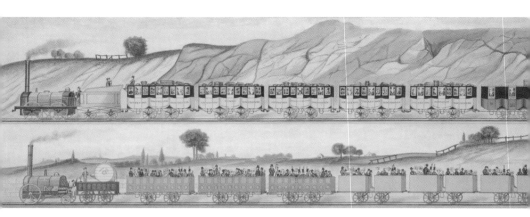

*Travelling on the Liverpool and Manchester Railway, 1831, by F. Broom. A second-class (unroofed) passenger train is shown below, with first class and the mail carriage above.*

Accidents were frequent on the new railways, including some to mail trains. On 6 March 1840, on the Carlisle & Newcastle Railway, 12 miles from Carlisle, a mail carriage was derailed by a line of laden coal wagons behind and was thrown over an embankment. The mail guard, Thomas Dougall, was killed, possibly the first fatality to a Post Office railway official.

By 1839 around 67 million letters were passing through the Post Office annually. Following postal reform in 1840, the reduced cost of postage and the introduction of the world's first postage stamp (the Penny Black) led to a rapid increase in mail volume. The growth of railways occurred at exactly the right time.

In 1844 there were 2,240 miles of railway; by 1853 there were 7,512 miles. The number of letters handled by the Post Office grew from 242 million to 411 million during the same period. Reliance solely on road-going vehicles could not continue if quality of service was to be maintained.

Railways at this time mostly linked the larger commercial centres. A large number of mail vans still had to be contracted to convey mail between post office and station, to complete long-distance routes not covered by rail, or to deliver mail to rural districts. The ratio of road to rail transport steadily altered and by the mid-nineteenth century more mail was being transported by rail than by road.

*Possibly the earliest surviving postmarked railway mail is this mis-sent item dated 13 June 1838, when the London & Birmingham Railway was not yet fully connected.*

While the public found railway travel was becoming less expensive than road transport, the Post Office experienced the opposite. In 1854 conveyance of night mail to the Potteries, Stone, Congleton and Macclesfield involved seven mail carts, a pair-horse van and two mail guards, costing £976 5s *per annum*. Using the North Staffordshire Railway would have required six mail carts, a night train between Stafford and Macclesfield and three station messengers, costing £1,582 11s 4d – a difference of £606 6s 4d. In these circumstances conveyance by road continued.

Preserved 'bracket box' at Llandrindod Wells station; these post boxes were produced by the Office of Works in the 1880s. Following the introduction of wall boxes from 1857, many were erected at railway stations, often following a railway company's request to the Post Office to improve station facilities.

To complement mail trains, improved posting facilities were installed wherever possible at stations. *The Times* reported in May 1849 that Post Office letter boxes were established at every 'first class' railway station. During the mail-coach era the Post Office had established 'forward' offices on their routes. These were distanced about every hundred miles or where they could best act as sorting and distributing offices for mail in that area. A similar practice continued with the railways. Forward or 'station' offices were established wherever they were best placed to complement the growing rail network. Important station offices were situated at Bletchley, Chester, Crewe, Derby, Ely, Gloucester, Normanton and Swindon, though there were many others.

As new railways opened, many were contracted to carry mail and incorporated into the Post Office's expanding distribution network, accelerating letter delivery. There was now frequently no need for letters to pass through the London offices, as many had done before the railways. Railway post offices travelling between Bristol and Exeter began in May 1847, and between Gloucester and Tamworth in July 1850. Tamworth then became the point at which mail from the West of England, Wales, Ireland and Scotland was concentrated for onward transmission to Yorkshire, Newcastle, northern and north-eastern England.

In 1849 Rowland Hill was keen to reduce the workforce required in the London Chief

South Western Sorting Tender handstamp. Sunday Sorting Tenders were introduced on 20 April 1850 on the Cambridge, Ipswich, Midland, Great Western, North Western, South Western and South Eastern lines.

HULL
A
15DE
72
SORTING-TENDER
Messrs. ROLLIT & SONS,
Solicitors,
HULL.

Letter bearing the Hull Sorting Tender postmark, 1872. Sorting Tenders were redesignated as Sorting Carrriages from 8 March 1904.

Office on Sundays. To achieve this, he introduced a new type of sorting carriage, called Sunday Sorting Tenders. These took in letters on their journeys *out* of London (the 'Down' journey) on Saturday and Sunday nights. This allowed sufficient time for onboard staff to sort whilst travelling in the opposite direction to which the letters were destined. Sorted mail was then transferred to an 'Up' train travelling *towards* London for onward despatch without increasing the time of delivery.

By 1853 mail was being carried on 206 lines belonging to sixty-two railway companies: thirty-eight in England and Wales, twelve in Scotland and twelve in Ireland. Much of this was simply the transit of a few mail bags in locked vans. The rate paid to each railway company varied enormously as

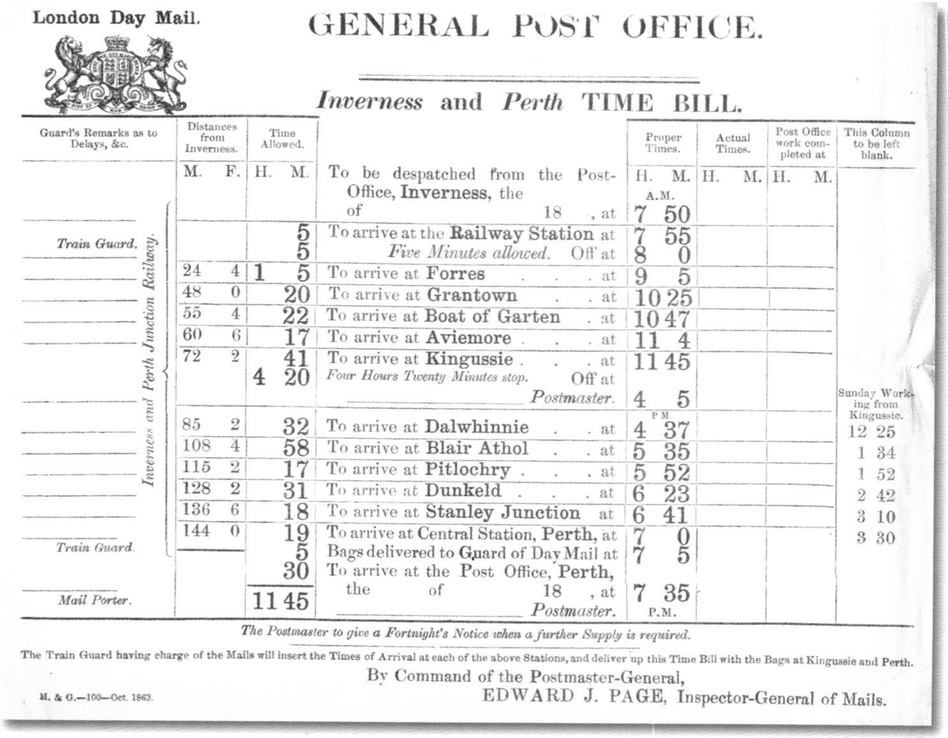

**London Day Mail.**

# GENERAL POST OFFICE.

## *Inverness* and *Perth* TIME BILL.

*Inverness and Perth Junction Railway.*

| Guard's Remarks as to Delays, &c. | Distances from Inverness. M. | F. | Time Allowed. H. | M. | | Proper Times. H. | M. | Actual Times. H. M. | Post Office work completed at H. M. | This Column to be left blank. |
|---|---|---|---|---|---|---|---|---|---|---|
| | | | | | To be despatched from the Post-Office, **Inverness**, the of 18 , at | A.M. 7 | 50 | | | |
| *Train Guard.* | | | | 5 | To arrive at the **Railway Station** at | 7 | 55 | | | |
| | | | | 5 | *Five Minutes allowed.* Off at | 8 | 0 | | | |
| | 24 | 4 | 1 | 5 | To arrive at **Forres** . . . at | 9 | 5 | | | |
| | 48 | 0 | | 20 | To arrive at **Grantown** . . at | 10 | 25 | | | |
| | 55 | 4 | | 22 | To arrive at **Boat of Garten** . at | 10 | 47 | | | |
| | 60 | 6 | | 17 | To arrive at **Aviemore** . . . at | 11 | 4 | | | |
| | 72 | 2 | | 41 | To arrive at **Kingussie** . . . at | 11 | 45 | | | |
| | | | 4 | 20 | *Four Hours Twenty Minutes stop.* Off at | | | | | |
| | | | | | *Postmaster.* | 4 | 5 | | | Sunday Working from Kingussie. |
| | 85 | 2 | | 32 | To arrive at **Dalwhinnie** . . at | P.M. 4 | 37 | | | 12 25 |
| | 108 | 4 | | 58 | To arrive at **Blair Athol** . . at | 5 | 35 | | | 1 34 |
| | 115 | 2 | | 17 | To arrive at **Pitlochry** . . . at | 5 | 52 | | | 1 52 |
| | 128 | 2 | | 31 | To arrive at **Dunkeld** . . . at | 6 | 23 | | | 2 42 |
| | 136 | 6 | | 18 | To arrive at **Stanley Junction** at | 6 | 41 | | | 3 10 |
| *Train Guard.* | 144 | 0 | | 19 | To arrive at Central Station, **Perth**, at | 7 | 0 | | | 3 30 |
| | | | | 5 | Bags delivered to Guard of Day Mail at | 7 | 5 | | | |
| | | | | 30 | To arrive at the Post Office, Perth, | | | | | |
| *Mail Porter.* | | | 11 | 45 | the of 18 , at *Postmaster.* | 7 | 35 P.M. | | | |

*The Postmaster to give a Fortnight's Notice when a further Supply is required.*

The Train Guard having charge of the Mails will insert the Times of Arrival at each of the above Stations, and deliver up this Time Bill with the Bags at Kingussie and Perth.

By Command of the Postmaster-General,
EDWARD J. PAGE, Inspector-General of Mails.

M. & G.—100—Oct. 1863.

General Post Office Inverness and Perth mail-train time-bill, 1863.

each drove a hard bargain and much depended on whether they ran a passenger service in conjunction with the mail service to keep costs down. To cite two extremes, in 1853 the Leeds Northern Railway charged ¼d per mile for carrying mail between Leeds and Ripley. The Chester & Holyhead Railway, however, charged 4s 10d per mile. In light of the expense, five years later the Government provided part of the Chester & Holyhead Railway's payment as a grant to 'increase general facilities for communication with Ireland'.

The Post Office was as much plagued by irregular train running as passengers. In 1854 a government select committee was appointed to investigate causes of irregularity in the conveyance of mails by railway. It quickly ascertained that numerous delays and other problems were occurring on all principal lines. Officials were quick to blame the railways despite the improvements in time that were being realised. For example, five

Moses Nobbs, former mail-coach guard, loading mails and newspapers on to an early railway post office, probably at Cannon Street Station.

railways were involved in running the night mail train from London via Derby and Newcastle to Edinburgh. In May 1853 night mails via this route reached Edinburgh at 14.20; the following month timetable changes shortened this by two hours.

With such a large number of independent railway companies involved, any delay was problematic. The time for transferring mail bags from train to train varied from five to thirty minutes, with little room for error.

In 1856 mail trains to the north were frequently late. In the last six months of the year 112 out of 368 mail trains were late. Following repeated complaints from the Post Office to the London & North Western, Lancaster & Carlisle and Caledonian railway companies, there was some improvement: only nine delays in the following six months. This was not enough for the Post Office, however, which pressed for the train to be run as a 'Special' – carrying mail without passengers. Such trains were run at just 25½ mph (including stoppages), so regularity was easier to sustain than on faster routes. These contrasted with 'Limited' mail trains, first suggested in 1858, which included a number of passenger carriages.

An express train introduced between London and Dover enabled London merchants to reply the same morning to letters from France received by the night mail. Letters arriving in London from Scotland, Ireland and the north and south-west of England by the day mail could also be sent on by day mail to Dover instead of being held back for the night mail train.

Until the mid-nineteenth century mail was exchanged only between head offices for distribution within a district. With the growing use of railways this was no longer necessary and, to accelerate the mail further, the Post Office decided to supply some offices directly. Where an office exchanged mail with a railway post office rather than through its head office, it became known as a railway sub-office, or RSO. These were not necessarily at or near a railway station. Hundreds of RSOs existed, even on islands that had no railway post office. The first office to be so designated was

The world's earliest dated railway-station postmark, on a letter sent from Bristol to Uckfield, Sussex. The 1d stamp is 'tied' by a Bristol Maltese Cross cancellation. On the rear is the double-arc cancellation 'GLOUCESTER/STATION', dated 19 March 1842.

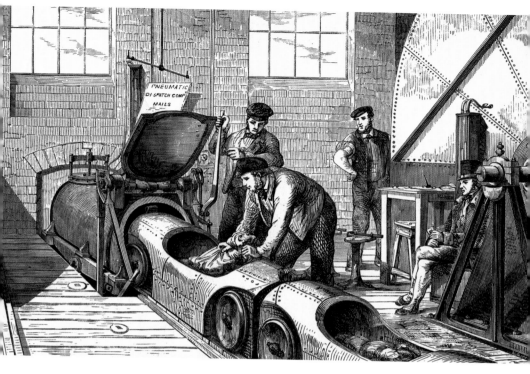

probably Braco in Perthshire in March 1856, though it was another ten years before RSOs were listed in the quarterly *Post Office Guide*.

In 1856 London was split into ten postal districts, each with its own district post office that acted as a Head Office. To simplify the circulation of letters, nine District Sorting Carriages were created between 1856 and 1863. These carriages sorted mail for London into direct bags for the districts whilst heading towards the city. However, within a decade it was decided that they were too expensive to operate.

While the number of railway companies carrying mail continued to increase rapidly, there were some exceptions: the day mail carried by the Dundalk & Enniskillen Railway was withdrawn in 1858 because the amount carried was too small to justify the payment demanded by the company. By 1859 a letter sent from Land's End to John O'Groats involved twenty-one separate contracts between the Post Office and the railway companies. The following year Post Office regional surveyors were 'encouraged' to look at the practicalities of sending mail by rail, and on 1 December 1860 they were instructed to send their superiors details of any railway which was not being employed for postal purposes, citing the reason.

The London Pneumatic Railway Despatch Company underground line began operation on 20 February 1863. Rail cars carried mail bags between Euston station and the post office at Eversholt Street, operated by means of a vacuum in one direction and compressed air in the other. The idea never found favour with the Post Office, which ceased using it in 1874.

# TRAVELLING POST OFFICES

RAILWAY POST OFFICES, carriages dedicated to sorting mail in transit, became known as travelling post offices, or TPOs. The term could refer interchangeably to a single dedicated sorting carriage or to a series of one or more sorting and stowage carriages and bag tenders; in later years the term could include the propelling vehicle. TPOs received mail at the start of their journey and at stations or bag-exchange points en route. Mail bags were opened by travelling postal staff, and the contents were sorted and included in new mail bags made up en route, and despatched at the appropriate station.

The important function TPOs provided was the facility to sort mail posted too late to be sorted in a stationary distributing or forwarding office. Post boxes were also incorporated into carriage exteriors, enabling the public to post late letters directly into TPOs at stations. Such letters required an additional 'late' fee.

Accelerated delivery was made possible by opening mail bags and sorting and despatching correspondence while the TPO was travelling towards the destination of the letter. Large numbers of mail bags could also be carried in accompanying stowage cars.

There were three main classes of mail carriage:

- Travelling post office: sorting carriage(s) under the control of the Chief Superintendent of TPOs.
- Sorting carriage/tender: sorting carriage(s) under the control of a provincial postmaster.
- Bag tender: carriage(s) set aside exclusively for the sorting or stowage of mail bags, and occasionally their receipt and despatch.

The layout of TPOs evolved quickly, driven by the work involved. Sorting frames (pigeonholes) were normally on the right (looking towards the engine). These had a well table below for emptying mailbags into. Protruding edges were padded to prevent injury. Fittings could include dedicated sorting frames for short letters, newspapers and packets, and registered letters. The last kind was fitted with a lockable roller shutter. Opposite the frames were rows of metal pegs, about 4cm apart, hung with bag labels in readiness for mail bags to be suspended from them.

Opposite:
Sorting on board the Great Northern TPO midday mail. This 56-foot sorting carriage was built in 1909. During the First World War it was lent to the Admiralty for naval service between Edinburgh and Inverness.

Because TPOs were a *moving* sorting office, the way mail was sorted on board altered during a journey. This alteration was accommodated by chalked marks, or later by the use of interchangeable strips called 'fillets', below each pigeonhole, according to the plan being sorted to. At a certain point on the journey sorting to that plan would cease, all letters in each pigeonhole would be tied up and deposited in prepared mail bags, and fillets (or chalk marks) changed; sorting then recommenced to a new plan. Bags from the previous plan would be tied up ready for deposit at the train's next stop.

Above: Postcard posted 'unpaid' into the Ipswich Sorting Tender Night Down, 1904. The sorting clerk has applied the tender's handstamp together with a 'POSTED WITHOUT LATE FEE' rubber stamp and manuscript '2', indicating the surcharge to be collected on delivery.

Right: Some earlier TPO mail-bag receiving nets were of the 'short form'. Pouches of mail had to be lifted into the carriage, an unpleasant procedure if wet or at night.

*Interior of Travelling Post Office*: poster design by George Charlton, commissioned by the Post Office Public Relations Department, 27 May 1935, but rejected by the Poster Advisory Group, 12 February 1936.

One of the most remarkable aspects of TPOs was the bag-exchange apparatus. This enabled mail trains to pass through stations of minor importance without stopping, yet still exchange mail bags. On some early

Coloured drawing of a 32-foot West Coast Joint Stock TPO showing the mail-bag exchange apparatus, November 1890.

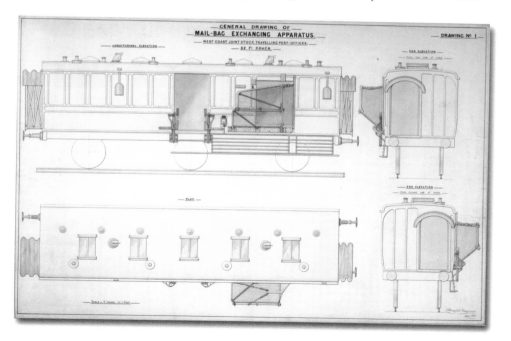

Engraving illustrating the perils of extending the mail-bag exchange apparatus at the wrong time.

'Fixing on' at the wayside mail-bag exchange apparatus, 1949.

TPOs bags were simply thrown out at a station as the locomotive steamed past, but the train could not easily receive bags in the same manner.

A bag-exchange apparatus was being fitted to some sorting carriages very early in their evolution. Following early trials, successful exchange of mail via apparatus took place at Boxmoor (Hemel Hempstead) in May 1838. Apparatus was erected at a handful of other sites and further improved in 1848. Two years later it was approved for general use across the country and by 1853 there were forty-two sites in operation. However, the Great Western Railway (on the advice of their engineer, I. K. Brunel) and the London & South Western Railway both resisted its introduction, citing the danger of such a mechanism. The former acquiesced in 1858, but the latter never gave way.

Mail bags transferred by apparatus were enclosed in protective leather pouches, the shock of transfer being absorbed by a rope net mounted on an iron frame. Trackside apparatus consisted of one or two despatching standards (or cranes) in conjunction with a ground net. These were erected in such a way that a passing TPO with its net apparatus extended would snatch any pouches suspended at the trackside, simultaneously despatching into the trackside net any pouches hung from the carriage. At many apparatus points both operations were carried out. Staff had to ensure pouches were not swung out too soon or too late. Pouches swung out too early might strike a bridge or other obstacle. Any presented for exchange too late would obviously miss the net.

At the start of a journey, a TPO acted mostly as a collecting office, receiving mail via the carriage. Later, it became more of a distributing office, with the bag apparatus delivery arms (tractors) used more often.

Because the transfer apparatus and pouches protruded from the side of the train, accidents occurred. In 1855 a Croydon railway messenger was killed when the trainside apparatus struck his head as he was preparing a mail bag for pickup: he was late on this occasion. Trackside nets were not to be lowered or pouches suspended more than fifteen minutes before a mail train was due. Until the train passed, it was not safe to approach or leave the standard except from behind the net frame.

Trackside apparatus was equally dangerous to train passengers. Between 1889 and 1891 four fatalities occurred, mostly caused by people leaning too far out of a carriage window. To reduce the danger, the trackside apparatus was moved further from the track at many sites.

In the mid- to late nineteenth-century most dedicated mail trains carrying postal staff on board were four- or six-wheeled carriages, primitive in design, with only basic facilities. Access between Post Office carriages was first possible from 1857, when the Midland Railway Company offered to provide them between the TPO and the mail-bag tender, though it took a number of years for the feature to become standard.

Trackside huts were provided as shelter from the weather and to store leather pouches for the mail bags. The small window at the rear enabled the apparatus messenger to see the approaching mail train.

The apparatus messenger climbing the adder to attach the mail pouch to the standard; it is swung away from the track for safety reasons. Pouches would not be swung out until just before the mail train was due.

Above: The 'Scotsman' exchanging mail pouches at between 50 and 60 mph. This photograph catches the exact moment pouches hanging from the carriage are snatched into the trackside delivery net. The trackside pouch is about to be caught by the carriage net just coming into shot from the right.

Above right: Collecting mail bags from inside the exchange pouches. Mail transferred by apparatus was enclosed in heavy leather pouches for protection.

In 1860 experiments to improve access between TPO carriages took place on the Great Western, South Eastern and London & North Western railways. Gangways used on the South Eastern Railway were designed and patented in 1864 by a Mr Landsdown. These were so successful that in November 1869 it was requested that all Post Office carriages be fitted with the 'Landsdown gangway', the Post Office paying royalties of 15s for each carriage end.

From the 1860s gradual improvements were made as new carriages replaced older ones. The low flat roofs, common to all carriages of the time, were replaced with arched ones. Ventilators were installed to remove 'vitiated air'; better lights were fitted; floor matting was provided, together with padding inside the carriage; and, for the first time, seats were placed in all TPOs. Connecting doorways (vestibules) between carriages were originally usually on the left and always on the side where mailbags were hung. Later TPOs had centrally located connecting doors between carriages to allow room for extra fittings such as a small kitchen.

Work on TPOs could be dangerous and demanding. In the nineteenth century fumes from oil lamps and melting wax (used for sealing bags) caused respiratory problems. However, staff were reluctant to take holidays because they would lose the extra payments made for each journey (trip allowance); there are accounts of officers working forty nights consecutively. An 1860 ruling decreed that staff should take two nights' rest after six nights' work. Also in the nineteenth century, large numbers of railway sorters were forced to retire owing to ailments 'attributed to the peculiar character of their duties'. These included 'Loss of Memory, Congestion of Brain and Spine,

An early Midland Railway 30-foot six-wheeled sorting carriage, no. 6, 1869, showing the off-set gangway.

Post Office staff beside the first North Eastern Railway coach, 1881. Six-wheeled carriage no. 1 is fitted with an early 'short-form' bag-exchange apparatus, and a 'late fee' post box hangs beside the door. Small chimneys on the side of the carriage were for venting the hot wax used to seal mail bags.

Paralysis' and 'Injury to Spine and Nervous System'. Safety was lacking in earlier years: between 1860 and 1867 there were twenty-eight serious accidents to forty-one clerks and seventy sorters working on TPOs; two postal staff were killed.

The locomotives used on mail trains were frequently the most powerful and renowned that a railway company had. The six-wheel 'singles' built by

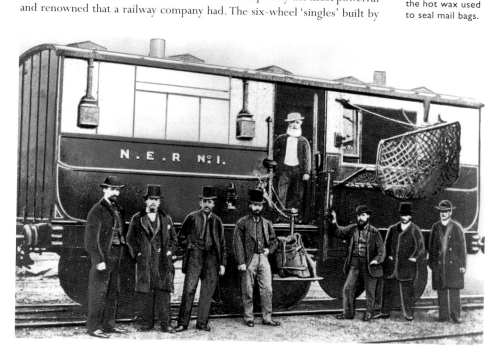

The Great Western Railway TPO Day Mail, c. 1890, running on broad-gauge tracks. This service was accelerated in 1869 by the installation of mail-bag exchange apparatus at Weston Junction.

James I'Anson Cudworth for the South Eastern Railway in the 1850s were used on the continental and express mail services so often that they became known as the 'Mails'. Supplanted by larger Cudworth engines the following decade, they transferred to the Hastings and Ramsgate routes, becoming known as the 'Little Mails'.

Twenty years after it first ran, the 'Irish Mail' suffered a horrific accident. The London & North Western Railway Down 'Irish Mail' left London Euston

Bag exchange by apparatus with the TPO normally took place away from public scrutiny. Visitors to Colwyn Bay would have found the spectacle of the passing 'Irish Mail' fascinating, making a fine subject for picture postcards.

for Holyhead at 07.30 on 20 August 1868. It consisted of a guard's van, mail van and bag tender, luggage van, four passenger carriages and a second guard's van at the rear. Four more passenger carriages were attached at Chester. Further along the line, part of a goods train was accidentally left to run off unattended towards Abergele – and the approaching mail train. The 'Irish Mail' ran into the wagons at 28–30 mph. The goods wagons were carrying fifty wooden barrels containing around 8,000 litres of paraffin oil. These burst and the contents were almost immediately ignited by the locomotive firebox. A fireball quickly engulfed the engine, tender, guard's van and three of the passenger carriages. Flames spread to the fourth and to the travelling post office. Luckily the Post Office workers managed to escape. The rear passenger carriages were detached but thirty-three deaths occurred. At the time it was the worst railway disaster in Britain and led to the introduction of 'catch points' on inclines to derail runaway vehicles.

One peculiar aspect of railway timetables related to the time. From the very beginning, many railway companies used 'London' time while also having to contend with a 'local' time that could vary by many minutes. This practice caused much confusion, resulting in missed trains and the potential for accidents. Some stopping stations were furnished with two clocks, or clocks with two minute-hands. Mail guards recorded 'GPO time' on their time-bills. The Statutes (Definition of Time) Act of 2 August 1880 introduced a standard time across the country.

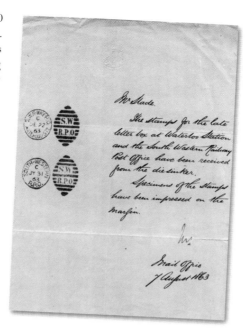

Impressions of handstamps issued in 1863 for use on late letters posted at Waterloo station. These were used at the station and on board the South Western Railway Post Office.

The London Midland & Scottish Railway 'Irish Mail' at Holyhead, 1925. The inspector hands the official watch to a postman, who will hand it to the officer in charge of the steam packet. The use of 'time-pieces', with time set at Post Office headquarters and locked to prevent tampering, continued a practice introduced with mail coaches.

# A NATIONAL NETWORK

IN 1883 the Post Office introduced a parcel post. Because the service relied heavily on railway infrastructure, the Treasury was prepared for the Post Office to pay half of gross parcels revenue to the railway companies for transport. However, because of their extensive experience in transporting parcels, and taking advantage of their strong position, the railways held out for more. Eventually 55 per cent of revenue was agreed. Consequently, not only did the railways carry the majority of Post Office parcels, receiving over 50 per cent of receipts *and* charging for transport, they also continued their own parcels service in competition. This did not please some senior Post Office officials, and a return was made to road transport on a number of routes, with large horse-drawn parcel coaches being introduced across the country.

The practicality of sorting parcels on the move was now considered. Under the Post Office (Parcels) Act, 1882, the Post Office was entitled to ask (or demand) any railway to provide, if required, in every ordinary train, a special parcels van or separate carriage in which parcels could be sorted. The majority of railway companies were approached in June 1883 regarding the provision of parcel post sorting vans; sorting en route first took place in July 1885. Carriage design varied across the nation. Apart from carriages converted from other use, the LNWR probably had the greatest range in sizes; LNWR 38 (built in 1885) was the smallest: at a mere 27 feet 6 inches, it was little more than half the length of LNWR 21 (built in 1898), which measured 50 feet. Payment for these vans was either agreed or settled by arbitration.

Huge numbers of newspapers were also carried and sorted on mail trains. Rail charges for carrying newspapers were particularly cheap, with bundles carried in parcel vans. Large numbers were also sent individually through the post. In 1888 newspaper sorters were supplied from the Newspaper Section of the Post Office's Circulation Office for sorting newspapers on board the TPOs. Exceptionally narrow and deep newspaper sorting frames were used. Sorters were expected to work with great accuracy and speed on the TPOs but were allowed more time for different classes of mail.

Opposite: Railex leaflet, 1937. Railex was introduced in the late 1930s to send urgent letters (up to 2 ounces in weight) to distant places as quickly as possible; senders took letters to a post office accepting express letters, which then sent them to the nearest railway station for despatch by the first available train. They were then collected and delivered at the other end by a messenger.

When the Post Office started its own parcel post in 1883, it soon became necessary to identify the mode of transport for revenue purposes. For many years a large handstamped 'COACH BORNE' or 'RAILWAY BORNE' mark was applied.

Following the Light Railways Act, 1896, there was a further, if smaller, expansion of railways throughout the country. Many light railways were used by the Post Office for small-scale mail carriage, frequently just a single bag containing a handful of letters. Two examples from north Kent are typical. The Sheppey Light Railway opened on 1 August 1901. The small Isle of Sheppey community made few demands on the postal service, as reflected by the Post Office's agreement to periodical payments for a steam Railmotor to convey just a single bag of mail between Queenborough and Eastchurch. Not 10 miles away, a Rainham to

Bristol, Shrewsbury and York TPO parcel carriage.

THE HIGHLAND MAIL (1,484 Feet Above Sea – Level).

The small 'Highland Mail' carriage provided an important service. This postcard shows it at Druimuachdar pass, 1,484 feet above sea level – the highest point on the railway network.

Many tramcars were used for conveying either post boxes or single bags of mail. From 1906 some Halifax trams hauled a mail wagon from the post office to the railway station. The station messenger travelled at the rear, watching for problems.

Chatham (from 1910) and Rochester (from 1917) mail bag was conveyed by tram over the Chatham & District Light Railway Company's line, the 4s a week cost for this service being paid for by the local postmaster.

In 1885 the Great Western Railway (GWR) and the Postmaster General had signed a contract for the purpose of carrying mail by rail. The total weight and number of mail bags had, however, steadily increased, leaving the railway

company feeling this had grown out of proportion to the fixed payment. The Postmaster General disagreed, believing the payment to be not only sufficient but comparatively high. Consequently, the GWR terminated the contract in 1899 and the dispute was taken to the Railway and Canal Commission. The outcome was the 1903 judgement, establishing:

Envelope recovered from the Grantham train disaster, 1906. Instead of stopping, the train ran through Grantham station at 40–50 mph; eleven passengers and a Post Office worker lost their lives. A faint 'DAMAGED AT GRANTHAM' handstamp has been applied to the envelope.

• Payment for conveyance of a mail bag set at the rate of a parcel, less some discounts for terminal services and relating to regularity.

• A lump sum was paid to the GWR to compensate it for loss of revenue stemming from subnormal running times of controlled trains.

• A lump sum was calculated for the GWR TPO Up and Down trains.

• A pence-per-mile payment was made to cover the construction, maintenance, lighting and haulage of sorting carriages. This varied according to carriage size.

• Post Office sorters' fares were paid at season ticket rates.

• Miscellaneous items were covered by a lump sum.

The influence of the 1903 judgement reverberated throughout the following years. It remained largely unchallenged and became the basis for most subsequent contracts between the Post Office and the railway companies and their successors, including the British Transport Commission and British Railways, until the 1960s.

Alongside the widespread use of contracted railways to carry the mail, the development of dedicated TPO carriages continued. By 1905 electricity was being used in both the London to Queenborough and the Carnforth to Whitehaven sorting carriages for lighting the carriages and heating the wax for sealing mail bags. Other facilities were also required. Men had fallen to their death or been severely injured whilst attempting to relieve themselves from the door of moving sorting carriages. When questions were asked in Parliament regarding the provision of lavatories, the reply was: 'Lavatory accommodation is being provided in certain new mail carriages now being constructed in Ireland but it is not proposed to provide it in carriages at present in use.' This referred to new carriages being built for the Dublin and Queenstown day mail service but water closets had been provided on some other routes experimentally in previous years.

Parcel sorting on the railways ceased in November 1915 as a result of the First World War, though it was not actually abolished until October

Opposite bottom: Postcard showing a wrecked mail train at Shrewsbury station. The LNWR 'North Mail' (the Bristol–Shrewsbury–York TPO) crashed on 15 October 1907. Eighteen people were killed and forty-four injured.

Left: British troops loading mail bags on to a Midland Railway carriage used for the Calais–Cologne TPO during the First World War.

Stamps and labels were produced by railway companies for the services they provided. Railway Letter Service stamps produced by the South Eastern Railway reflect an almost generic design shared by many United Kingdom railways. 'Farm produce' labels produced for the South Eastern & Chatham & Dover Railway saw relatively little use, unlike the 'newspaper' labels supplied by the South Eastern & Chatham Railway. Parcel labels were cheaply printed and more suited to being pasted on to large, possibly irregularly shaped parcels.

1922, the Post Office having finally realised that the cost of sorting parcels on the railways was prohibitive. Those companies being paid to construct parcel-sorting carriages were advised they would no longer be required for this purpose.

Before the First World War there were more than 130 TPOs in use. When the Government took control of the railways, some TPOs were suspended as part of the wartime economy. In addition, from 29 September to 2 October 1919 the nation suffered a national railway strike over an agreement to standardise wages. This forced the Post Office to

A 1911 express letter sent via the Railway Letter Service, with instructions for it to catch the 2.15 Great Eastern Railway train to Broxbourne. On arrival it would have been handed to a Post Office messenger for immediate delivery.

seek alternative transport for mail, both inland and to the continent, via commercial air services.

Inland air-mail charges were, however, set very high: letters had to bear the usual rate of postage plus a special fee of 2s per ounce, and after the strike the press accused the Post Office of profiting from it. Though it was a valuable exercise in logistics, the experience did little to convince the Post Office to move permanently from rail to air.

Following the Railways Act 1921, the 'Grouping' occurred on 1 January 1923. This brought together the majority of the railway companies to form the 'Big Four': the Great Western Railway (GWR), the London Midland & Scottish Railway (LMS), the London & North Eastern Railway (LNER), and the Southern Railway (SR). Each of these continued to vie for Post Office traffic.

The period before the Second World War was the heyday of the day mail TPOs. Although fewer in number, they left King's Cross, Liverpool Street, Waterloo and Paddington and provided onward conveyance for the night mails that had recently arrived in London. Up day TPOs bringing mails into London connected with Down night mails.

E. ☂ R.
This Packet has been diverted from the usual route, as it appeared to be too fragile for transfer by the Mail Apparatus.

M.—No. 10.
Date Stamp.

Between 1902 and 1930 special labels were pasted on to items thought too fragile to withstand the considerable shock of being exchanged by apparatus.

'Night Mail' poster design by Pat Keely, 1939, for the 1936 GPO film of the same name.

'Night Mail' poster design by 'ART' (Alfred Reginald Thomson), 1937.

33

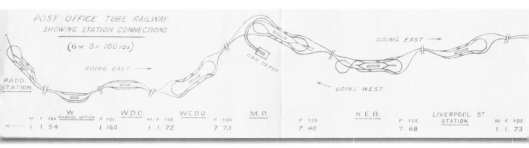

POST OFFICE TUBE RAILWAY
SHOWING STATION CONNECTIONS.
(6M 3F 100YDS)

GOING EAST →

GOING EAST →

CAR DEPOT

← GOING WEST.

PADD.
STATION

| W PARCEL OFFICE | W.D.O. | WC.D.O. | M.P. | K.E.B. | LIVERPOOL ST STATION | |
|---|---|---|---|---|---|---|
| M. F. YDS | F. YDS | M. F. YDS | F. YDS | F. YDS | F. YDS | F. YDS | M. F. YDS |
| 1. 1. 54 | 1. 160 | 1. 1. 72 | 7. 73 | 7. 40 | 7. 68 | 1. 1. 73 |

← 

Map of the Post Office Underground Railway, showing eight stations and interconnecting lines. The car depot for repairs and maintenance at Mount Pleasant is shown in the centre.

The number of mail-bag exchange apparatus points was probably at its highest in 1913, when 245 were in use. By 1927 the 160 apparatus exchange points in Great Britain were involved in two hundred exchanges every twenty-four hours – transferring nearly 10 tons of mail. By 1934 this was reduced to 132 points, about forty of which were on the route of the London–Aberdeen Down Special TPO. The number of apparatus points continued to decrease, with just eighty-eight in use by 1936.

As TPOs reached their peak, another means of transporting mail by rail came into being: the Post Office Underground Railway. By the start of the twentieth century, congested streets and fog were severely delaying the transport of mail between the main post offices and railway stations in

Loading mail bags on to the Post Office Underground Railway. The chute down which they slide from the sorting office above can be seen on the left.

London. A committee was set up in 1909 to study the use of underground pneumatic and electric railways and in February 1911 recommended construction of an electric railway with driverless trains.

Tunnel construction began in 1914 and was completed in 1917, but the Treasury would not allow the Post Office to order or install equipment during wartime. During the First World War the unfinished tunnels were used to store paintings from some of London's museums and galleries. The first stretch of railway eventually opened on 5 December 1927, with parcels traffic running between Mount Pleasant and Paddington. When finally complete in 1928 the line had eight stations and ran for 6½ miles, connecting Paddington station in the west with Liverpool Street station in the east, calling at major post offices en route. With its own team of staff to transfer mails, the fully automated, driverless trains operated for twenty-two hours a day, stopping only for a brief daily period so that maintenance could be carried out.

By the 1930s a night mail TPO network covered Britain, complemented by several day mail services over some routes. Post towns were now being supplied with their mail through 'County Distributing Offices' (introduced in the 1920s). This new method of mail circulation simplified the complex arrangements that had been in place in land-based mail-distributing offices and on TPOs. This reduction in mail work enabled the cessation of the day mail rail services after the Second World War.

Transferring the mail from ship's tender to Great Western Railway train via an electrically operated conveyor at Plymouth docks. A 'King' or 'Castle' Class 4-6-0 express locomotive would reach Paddington, London, in about four hours.

# POST-WAR CHANGE

DURING THE Second World War mail volumes carried by rail increased. Letters were essential for maintaining morale and connecting families separated by wartime. The rail network carried immense quantities of mail: in 1943 British railways carried 25 million mail bags and over 90 million parcels.

Enemy bombing was often targeted on the transport network, frequently affecting postal operations. Following a raid on the night of 16/17 April 1941, London termini at Cannon Street, Holborn Viaduct, Charing Cross, Victoria, Waterloo, Paddington and Liverpool Street were briefly out of action, mostly because of damaged tracks beyond. Following such events, mail was delayed or transferred to road services, though damage was occasionally severe, as with the thirty bags of parcels destroyed by fire at Paddington station in February 1944.

After the Second World War changes in postal circulation ruled out the need for the day mail TPOs, and only forty-six of the seventy-seven pre-war TPOs were restored to service, mostly in October 1945. Four TPOs were special trains devoted entirely to Post Office work:

- Down Special TPO (London–Aberdeen)
- Up Special TPO (Aberdeen–London)
- Great Western TPO Down (London–Penzance)
- Great Western TPO Up (Penzance–London)

These were the names by which the trains were known in the Post Office, but railway officials referred to them as the 'Down Postal' and the 'Up Postal'. In its heyday the Up Special Travelling Post Office could, from Carlisle, consist of six sorting carriages and eleven letter and parcel stowage vans – the longest TPO train in the world. As many as fifty men could be working on this train. Conversely, local services might consist of a single carriage. Post Office staff on board, previously known as sorters, or railway clerks when TPOs were in their infancy, were now titled 'Postmen Higher Grade'.

Opposite:
Poster advertising the need for good timekeeping; unknown artist, 1962.

Loading mail bags at night on to the Down Special on the London Midland & Scottish Railway at Crewe station, 1934. Timekeeping was critical and the transfer of mail bags to and from TPOs was a finely honed operation.

Owing to the war, TPOs ceased to run in September 1940. The Great Western and the Up and Down Special TPOs were restored to service on 1 October 1945. The train that inaugurated the Great Western TPO Down service is shown here at Old Oak Common sidings, 1945.

In addition to multiple routes crossing the country, other principal TPOs running in both directions included:

- North Eastern TPOs: King's Cross–Edinburgh
- Midland TPOs: Bristol–Newcastle upon Tyne
- South Wales TPOs: Bristol–Carmarthen
- South Western TPOs: London–Weymouth
- Highland TPOs: Perth–Inverness
- East Anglian TPOs: London–Norwich

An electric truck loaded with mail bags at Chester railway station, 1934.

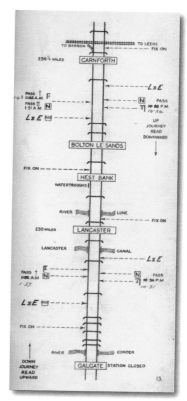

Part of the route of the Down/Up Special TPO. Instructions are provided showing when mail bags are loaded, despatched and received via the apparatus.

A major point of interchange was Crewe, where within two and a half hours eleven TPOs arrived and departed. These came from London, Aberdeen, Bangor, Birmingham, Cardiff, Carlisle, Glasgow, Lincoln, Peterborough, Shrewsbury and York. Bristol Temple Meads also became a major meeting point, with four TPOs exchanging mail there.

At a time when there were two or more deliveries of mail each day, the principal Down Night TPOs working out of London were timed to enable mail transported by rail to be included with the first delivery in England and Wales and, whenever possible, a next-day delivery in Scotland of mail that had been included in evening postings in London. Up Night services from the provinces to London were timed to connect with the first delivery in London districts and other nearby places. Cross-country and feeder TPOs connected with main routes to provide countrywide TPO coverage, which helped ensure next-day delivery nationwide. By this means, by the time a TPO reached its destination, most mail being sorted inside had been tied into bundles destined for individual post offices, with mail occasionally subdivided still further.

Reliable timekeeping was essential; if a train was late, then mail could miss connections to multiple destinations. Mail leaving London via the Great Western TPO Down could secure a first delivery throughout the West Country. Mail reached the first delivery in South Wales via connections with the South Wales TPO Down, and parts of the Midlands via the Bristol–Derby TPO. Letters from South Wales and the Midlands could also be transferred to the Great Western TPO Down at Bristol for onward conveyance to the West Country.

Because TPOs acted as mobile distribution offices for the counties they were approaching, sorting changed as they proceeded on their journey. On the Great Western TPO Down, letters for Somerset, Gloucestershire, Herefordshire and South Wales had to be completed by arrival at Bristol, those for Devon by arrival at Exeter, and those for Cornwall by arrival at Plymouth.

One gap in national mail-train coverage was East Anglia. In the late 1940s experiments were held to fill this gap with a helicopter service taking mail

Sorting letters on the Great Western Down. New rolling stock photographed at Paddington in 1960.

British Railways Midland Region sorting carriage no. 30309, built in 1950; photographed in 1958. This was the first carriage fitted with flourescent lighting.

on a round trip from Peterborough with fourteen stops, but it proved too expensive to maintain.

The design and construction of TPO carriages varied across the country. Until 1937 it had been the practice for provincial head postmasters to consult the Chief Superintendent TPO Section when instigating new carriage construction outside the control of London. Despite this, there remained a

The Up Special, built in 1968, en route to sidings; photographed on 31 January 1969.

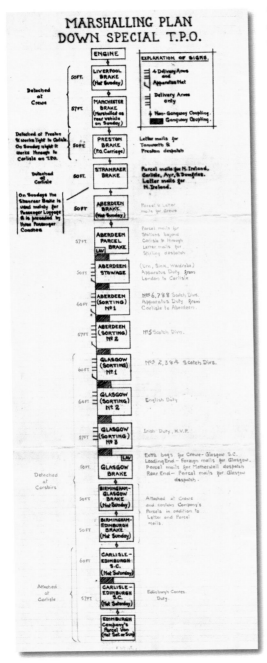

tendency to construct carriages specifically for the service they were required for. Local restrictions also affected the build of some carriages.

With the cessation of many services after the war, notably the day mails, it was found that many of the now spare carriages were of little use as general-purpose vehicles. The roster of sorting carriages records lengths varying from 44 to 70 feet. Widths varied from 8 to 9 feet. Width combined with length occasionally created problems of 'throw' (overhang) on curves. Consequently, some carriages were scrapped because of unsuitability and age.

Stowage vans took the place of guard or luggage accommodation used for mail on non-TPO trains. Lengths varied from 42 to 60 feet, width from 8 to 9 feet. The only stowage vans used for apparatus working were on the Down and Up Special TPOs and the Great Western TPOs.

The Transport Act 1947 nationalised the Big Four railway companies, bringing them under the control of a newly established British Transport Commission. This created a new national rail-operating company, British Railways, on 1 January 1948. Subsequently British Railways, trading as British Rail (BR), operated most of the country's rail operations until their privatisation in 1997. BR inherited a mixed bag of rolling stock in a variety of regional liveries and for the next few years broadly followed the LMS pattern for new postal carriages built at Wolverton. Security cages were fitted in ordinary sorting carriages in 1954, the Post Office paying around a quarter of the cost of these alterations.

During the late 1940s consideration was given to how best to standardise new-build TPO carriages. This led to a joint British

Opposite page:
Marshalling plan
for the Down
Special TPO. This
shows the
different sorting
duties undertaken
in each carriage on
different days of
the week. Only the
central carriages
were provided
with gangways.

Left: Mail bags
stowed in a
Down Special
TPO baggage
car in 1947.

Transport Commission/Post Office report in 1954. Two basic types of sorting carriage were required: either with or without bag-exchange apparatus. A lavatory could be provided in each of these types, and an electric oven and hot-water urn had become standard provision. Carriage lengths were standardised as far as possible.

Below: The Up
Special at Shap
Wells, 1961; the
net lights are
on as night falls.

Staff facilities on TPOs were basic. Post Office staff frequently had to wait one and a half hours into a journey before water was hot enough to make tea. The small oven was suitable only for heating a few pies or something similar. Mark I TPO No. 80306, built in 1959.

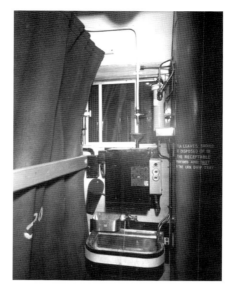

The Aberdeen–Carstairs portion of the Up Special photographed in 1964 at Carmuirs West Junction. The locomotive is A4 Class no. 60016, *Silver King*.

In 1951 the first Mark I range of BR coaches entered service, the first Mark I TPO stock being introduced in 1959. These new sorting carriages were fitted with better insulation and electrically operated gangway doors worked by a shoulder-height push button that could be operated by a man laden with mail bags. The first TPO carriage (old-style) fitted with fluorescent strip lighting in 1958 was also the last one built with an off-centre gangway. One immediate advantage of Mark I postal carriages was the use of standard, central gangways. Earlier carriages from the Western Region could not be gangwayed with vehicles from the London Midland, Eastern or North Eastern regions because of a difference in height of gangways and width of vestibules.

Further changes to mail trains came in response to external events. There had been robberies from mail trains since their inception. Most were relatively minor and frequently opportunist. However, one of the most notorious events involving a TPO occurred on 8 August 1963. The Glasgow to London Euston Up Special TPO was stopped at Sears Crossing between Leighton Buzzard and Cheddington and robbed. The twelve carriages, complete with seventy-two postal staff, were carrying a large quantity of high-value packets, almost all in the second carriage. Contents included registered parcels and an exceptional amount of money: the thieves escaped with around £2.6 million. Many of the gang were apprehended and received long prison sentences, but the repercussions for the Post Office of what became known as the 'Great Train Robbery' were long lasting.

A review of security on mail trains followed. Mail was being conveyed in guard's vans on twenty-three non-TPO routes: this ceased. The Post Office paid for additional security fittings to be provided on stowage vans and sorting carriages. Resulting alterations included: conversion from fourteen- to sixteen-gauge panels, coupling locking devices, steel underlining to floors, steel interior lining, additional dynamo and regulator, and provision for fitting loud hailers and VHF radio.

The Great Train Robbery may, however, have led to a new lease of life for TPOs. When the work to strengthen the carriages was considered, it became apparent that many were too old or fragile. It was proposed that BR provide twelve new, purpose-built, high-security TPO carriages, though just three were initially built (converted from old stock). Police officers accompanied many mail trains for years afterwards, but the days of trains carrying high-value packets were numbered and the practice ceased in the 1970s.

Retrieved high-value packets, torn open and discarded, and used as evidence in the trial of those apprehended for the Great Train Robbery, 8 August 1963.

The principles underlying the Post Office's contractual relationship with BR remained those established by the 1903 Great Western judgement. For decades the Post Office remained reluctant to reopen negotiations about payments for fear of being disadvantaged. By the mid-1960s payments for rail conveyance of letter mail were based on four main-line contracts, with supplementary agreements plus a number of minor contracts. The four main-line contracts and their start dates were: Great Western Railway (1928); Southern Railway, London & North Eastern Railway and London Midland & Scottish Railway (1930). From 1 July 1968 a further agreement came into effect under which all payments formerly dealt with separately were consolidated into one payment to the British Railways Board. This was necessary because of the loss of rail services available to the Post Office following the line closures resulting from the Beeching Report.

The Post Office had been a government department during the railway age and rail had been a natural progression for transporting mail. Nationwide rail coverage had grown and by the end of the nineteenth century there were few parts of the nation that the Post Office could not reach by rail. The 1963 Beeching Report, *The Reshaping of British Railways*, led to wide changes. Over 4,000 route miles of railway were closed on grounds of efficiency. This led the Post Office, a public corporation from 1969, to consider its options. Subsequently, the amount of mail routed through London increased as a result of the loss of cross-country routes. By 1973–4 it was calculated that one letter bag in every three entered or passed through London.

Above: An Ayr–Kilmarnock– Carlisle mail train photographed at Barassie, North Ayrshire, 1966. The locomotive is BR Standard Class 3MT no. 77019.

Opposite: Still from the film *Thieves Junction*, 1982. Directed by Eric Marquis with script by Christopher Cooke, this Post Office film aimed to raise staff awareness of the security of mail carried by rail.

Station stopping times on many inner suburban routes had become inadequate, with some halts in the Southern Region down to just thirty seconds. Since the duration of the station stop determined the number of bags that could be loaded and unloaded, this meant spreading some despatches over a number of trains. The Post Office found this intolerable and many road services were introduced to plug gaps.

Alongside the wider network of trains transporting mail, TPOs had evolved into a relatively small but efficient part of the nationwide mail-by-rail operation.

The 'Irish Mail' in charge of 'Britannia' Class Pacific no. 70047, photographed in 1968.

When two-tier post was introduced in 1968 it made sense for TPOs to carry only first-class letters, because second-class mail was not supposed to be delivered until the second working day and speed was not a necessity. The function of the TPOs, whether attached to, or forming, overnight trains, became to speed first-class letters, invariably posted quite late in the day, over mostly long distances. Consequently, the amount of work on TPOs began to reduce.

British Railways parcels ticket from Cardiff General, 1959.

The Ayr–Carlisle sorting carriage; a southbound parcels train at Bowhouse on the Nith Valley line in 1964. The locomotive is 'Britannia' Class no. 70006 *Robert Burns*.

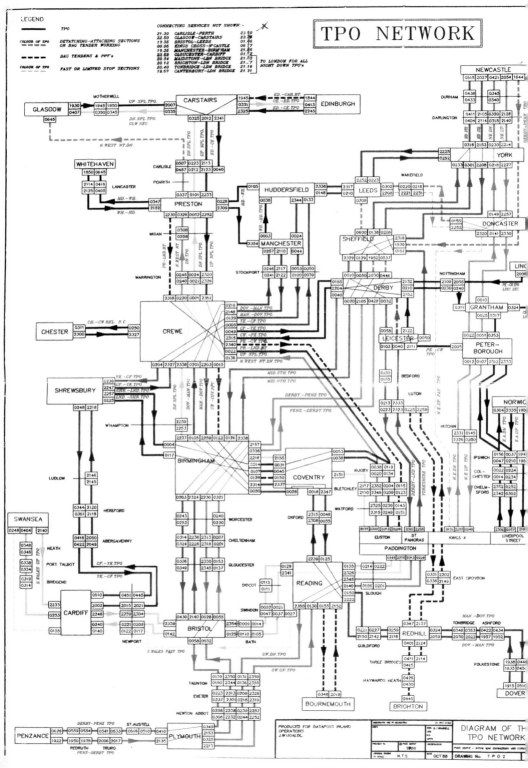

# TPO NETWORK

DIAGRAM OF THE TPO NETWORK

# MODERN MAIL TRAINS

IN THE LATE 1960s the Post Office's Parcel Post Plan concentrated parcel sorting into largely mechanised parcel concentration offices. To accommodate this, on 5 May 1969 BR introduced dedicated express parcels trains, operating at 90 mph, linking Bradford, Nottingham, Birmingham, Bristol and Cardiff. By the end of 1970, additional routes enabled the express parcels train system to link all the parcel concentration offices.

However, because the Post Office believed the transport arrangements did not suit the new network of parcel concentration offices, it did not seek long-term renewal of its parcels contract with BR after 1974. Instead, it implemented a combination of Post Office road vehicles, contract road services, Freightliner trains and conventional trains. The Post Office wished to increase its control over parcel-post movement, reduce handling, increase flexibility and ultimately reduce costs.

A Letter Post Plan similarly sought efficiency by concentrating the national letter flow into large mechanised letter sorting offices. This relied on the introduction of postcodes and a review of road and rail transportation, putting the future of TPOs in doubt. As one Post Office document expressed it, 'While it is not expected that mechanisation will have any marked effect on the work of the TPOs in the immediate future, their role will be steadily reduced.'

Use of the Post Office's own underground railway in London also declined in the 1960s and 1970s. Reduced mail traffic through London led to the cessation of a third delivery in central London in September 1972. Nevertheless, in 1972 the nation's railways earned nearly £74 million from carrying BR, Post Office and other national carriers' parcels, letters and newspapers.

By 1972 there were 102 sorting carriages and forty-four stowage vehicles. These covered 8 million miles annually, carrying 7 million mail bags. Additionally, around 412 million first-class letters and packets were being received, sorted and despatched each year from TPOs.

However, the majority of mail carried by rail travelled relatively short distances. In 1972 about 50 per cent of letters travelled less than 60 miles,

Opposite:
Map of the TPO network, 1988. London termini were still in use at this date.

51

British Rail Red Star Parcels leaflet. Introduced in 1963, Red Star was an express registered parcels service that competed with the Post Office until its cessation in 1995. By the 1980s five million Red Star parcels were being carried on trains each year.

Below right: Filling mail bags on the Paddington to Bristol TPO, 1980.

Below: By 1976 the late fee payable on items of mail posted directly into sorting carriages had been largely abolished, though the posting facility remained. This trainside letter box and its immediate surround are painted in British Rail 'flame red'.

37 per cent less than 100 miles, and most of the remainder less than 200 miles. Because conveyance by rail typically involved expensive extra handling, the Post Office sought cheaper road alternatives.

Industrial troubles plagued the nation in spring 1973, leaving the Post Office handicapped by enforced rail delays. Post Office claims against BR for delays between January 1972 and February 1974 amounted to £2,332,052. In the meantime, BR launched a counter claim for £450,000 relating to what it believed to be underpayment for the conveyance of parcels during 1969–70. The relationship was souring and where possible the Post Office decreased its reliance on the railways: a withdrawal programme was instigated.

In 1975 the Post Office was using ten thousand trains daily to transport mail, including 104 sorting carriages and forty-five stowage vans forming TPOs. TPOs covered 8.7 million miles and cost the Post Office over £3 million annually. Some of these were attached to ordinary passenger trains but there were also four complete postal trains: two between London and Scotland and two between London and Penzance. The 575 postal staff employed on any weekday covered 38.3 million miles in the trains annually. The cost of acceleration by TPO was about 1.6p per item of mail. 450 million first-class letters and packets were handled, and hundreds of thousands of mail bags were carried as stowage mail. Approximately 75 per cent of letter mails were carried by rail at some stage in their journey. Nevertheless, the suspension of Sunday mail collections from May 1976 led to the end of TPO Sunday working.

In December 1977 postal officials used the threat of transferring first- and second-class letters to air transport between London and Edinburgh and Newcastle in an attempt to improve the service on the East Coast Main Line.

Transfer of Datapost from a British Rail guard's van to a postman for local transport by road at Reading.

Sorting on board a BR blue-and-grey liveried TPO at Euston station prior to departure, 1981.

A postwoman
loads a TPO at
Crewe, 1988.

In February 1978 BR began replacing locomotive-hauled passenger trains on this line with new high-speed diesel trains (HSTs) but the Post Office calculated that moving mail via the new service would cost two and a half times more than the existing arrangement by air. Despite some services being accelerated, the Post Office was wary of new problems; costs of staff and equipment at stations rose owing to limited capacity on the new trains, and general quality of service fell in some regions as conventional, slower trains were cut out when timetables were altered.

Loading a BR blue-
and-grey liveried
TPO at Euston
station, 1981.

In 1979 the Post Office introduced an integrated inland air network centred on Speke (now John Lennon) Airport, Liverpool. 'Spokes of Speke' was joined by another hub at East Midlands Airport in 1982. The aim was to link air, rail and road transport. More direct air routes were introduced in

1992 and by the late 1990s these were carrying over 3 million items of mail every night.

Nevertheless, moving mail by rail retained advantages. Many sorting offices had been built next to railway stations. BR had the capacity and expertise to handle wide fluctuations in mail volumes, particularly at Christmas time, and rail remained the most advantageous mode of transport for urgent or first-class mail over middle-distance trunk routes. There remained the facility to use almost any passenger train in BR's network, and the TPO network remained a valued service for many first-class letters. Despite these advantages, disruption to mail delivery by rail delays remained a problem.

When the contract with BR expired on 31 March 1981, it was extended by mutual agreement pending negotiation. The Post Office was again permitted to use any passenger or parcels trains in the BR daily network. In practice this meant around 200,000 mail bags, or two-thirds of all letters posted, were carried each day on about four thousand of sixteen thousand available trains. These were 'Schedule II' services. 'Schedule I' services were 'controlled trains': 155 of these ran on main lines, about a third of which were TPOs.

The Post Office continued to make changes to mail circulation in the United Kingdom by making greater use of mail concentration offices and air services.

A TPO photographed between Bedford and Leicester, 20 September 1986, showing the new all-red livery, complete with red roofs (later changed to black), hauled by a Class 47 locomotive, no. 47515, *Night Mail*.

Class 47 locomotive and propelling control vehicle inside Princess Royal Distribution Centre, July 1996. RES locomotive names frequently began with or featured the letters RES. The fleet included *Rail Express Systems, Resounding, Respected, Resourceful* and *Resilient* (shown here).

Train timetable rehearsals at Princess Royal Distribution Centre, 8 December 1996.

The TPO network underwent changes to adapt to the new requirements and many routes were altered or dropped. Royal Mail Parcels transferred over 80 per cent of their parcels to road. In the early 1990s, virtually all Saturday movement of letters and packets transferred from rail to road under a Royal Mail scheme named 'Roadrunner'.

The railways' mail operation had become run down. However, Royal Mail invested £150 million into a new 'Railnet' partnership with BR's light

freight business, Rail Express Systems (RES). Using Railtrack's rail network, this aimed to get 100 million more letters delivered the day after posting. It was the biggest mail-moving change in Royal Mail's history. The ten-year agreement set high standards for performance and security. Maximum payments to the railways doubled, and Royal Mail committed to building a new 15-acre road/rail hub at Stonebridge Park in north London (later renamed Princess Royal Distribution Centre). This replaced Royal Mail operations at five London main-line stations – King's Cross, St Pancras, Liverpool Street, Paddington and Euston.

A new fleet of sixteen mail trains was commissioned. These were the Class 325 electric multiple units (EMUs) built by ABB Derby during 1995–6. These new trains were the first to be directly owned by Royal Mail and were built to exact requirements. The Class 325 four-car sets were capable of running from overhead electricity, third-rail electricity or being hauled by a locomotive. They could travel at 100 mph. A simplified rail network was devised for the new integrated service. Mail trains worked primarily on what had long been the Post Office's traditional and preferred route to the north: the West Coast Main line, linking London (PRDC), the Midlands, north-west England and Scotland. New hubs were opened at Bristol, Doncaster, Glasgow, Newcastle, Peterborough, Stafford and Warrington. Sixty BR stations formed part of Railnet and were provided with mail-container handling equipment.

Electric 'six-York movers' transport containerised mail on the platform at Princess Royal Distribution Centre, July 2010. 'Yorks', so called because they were developed in that city, travelled in sealed Class 325 electric multiple units with no postal staff on board.

By October 1995 around 450 vehicles had improved internal lighting, and most had tread-plate flooring and roller shutter doors fitted. To reflect the comprehensive refurbishment of the mail fleet, Rail Express Systems' diesel locomotive fleet was re-designated. Long-range fuel tanks were installed and driving cabs modernised. Reclassified Class 47/7, they were drawn from existing Class 47 stock.

In 1996 RES freight operations in the United Kingdom were purchased by Wisconsin Central, trading as English, Welsh & Scottish Railway (EWS). They inherited an ageing rail fleet consisting largely of Class 47 diesel and Class 86 electric locomotives. EWS recognised the need for modern,

A major change implemented with Railnet was the containerisation of letter mail. Wheeled containers holding mail in trays replaced mail bags. All mail trains were converted to accept these new 'York' containers. Each set of four carriages could fit 180 'Yorks'. No sorting took place on these trains – carriages were locked and sent to their destination.

fast locomotives to work the mail services, and a high-speed diesel replacement for the Class 47/7 was sought. A contract for thirty Class 67 locomotives was placed with General Motors, subcontracted to Alstom in Spain. These entered service in Britain in 2000 and were soon deployed on Royal Mail duties. Some of the locomotives were given names reflecting their duties, such as *Night Mail* (67001), *Special*

With no room for movement, 'mail order returns' have been loaded on to a Class 325 mail train. Yellow destination labels accompanied each 'York' cage, July 2010.

*Delivery* (67002) and *Post Haste* (67004), though the class was often referred to as 'Skips', a nickname based on their shape.

In 2000, following a passenger-train derailment at Hatfield, Railtrack imposed speed restrictions on several mail routes, and even complete closure of some. Enforced maintenance of the rail network followed, which, coupled with severe flooding in Scotland, led to twenty-seven mail trains being disrupted, delayed from between thirty minutes and six hours. Trains missed connections and letters were delivered late. Subsequently, Royal Mail thought hard about future railway dependence.

A Scottish crown (based on the St Andrew's Crown) on a Class 325 brake vehicle. Scottish-liveried carriages were used both north and south of the border.

By 2003 Royal Mail and EWS were operating forty-nine daily train services, of which sixteen were TPOs. These carried 20 million items of mail (about 14 per cent of the nation's postbag), including a quarter of all first-class mail. EWS stated that the performance of these trains exceeded that of any mainland passenger operator.

A revision of mail-routing operations, however, led to considerable mail volumes being transferred to air and road services. After two years of negotiation between Royal Mail and EWS, they had failed to reach agreement; this, coupled with rising concern over the health and safety of TPO staff, sealed the fate of TPOs.

EWS electro-diesel Class 73/1 no. 73131 passing through Kensington Olympia station at the rear of the Willesden to Dover mail, 30 July 1999.

The striking livery of the 'Ladies in Red', as the TPOs were known.

The United Kingdom had pioneered TPOs and the practice of sorting mail on the move. Nevertheless, the future for TPOs in Britain had been in doubt for decades and in June 2003 Royal Mail announced that it intended changing its entire rail-based distribution network to a road alternative, though it did not rule out a future return to rail. Following a phased withdrawal, the final TPO services ran on the night of 9 January 2004.

London's Princess Royal Distribution Centre remained open for distributing bulk mail, partly for rail but mostly for road operations. EWS's expensive Class 67s were left without the work for which they were built, and, despite redeployment, many simply went into storage.

By the end of December 2004, Royal Mail resumed small-scale movement with Christmas mail in closed rail carriages and, following successful trials, Royal Mail contracted GBRailfreight for at least two nightly services, transporting around one million letters a day. The contract was

The last night of operation for the TPO service photographed at Cheltenham, 8–9 January 2004.

flexible enough to allow for specials to run at peak times such as Christmas. Northbound and southbound services were operated on the West Coast Main Line though occasional use was made of the East Coast Main Line when necessary. Royal Mail's own Class 325 four-car sets were used, supplemented by locomotive haulage when required.

Some movement of parcels had continued unabated. EWS was still running its own daily express parcels service from Aberdeen to Walsall. By mid-2006 courier DHL was sending 75 per cent of its parcel business for Inverness via EWS. EWS was acquired by Deutsche Bahn AG in June 2007. On 1 January 2009 EWS, Railion and freight logistics company Schenker AG were rebranded as DB Schenker.

On 1 June 2010 Royal Mail awarded DB Schenker the contract to run up to seven rail services each day between Princess Royal Distribution Centre, Warrington and Glasgow, though only one was required at the outset. DB Schenker was responsible not only for operating the service, but also for the maintenance of Royal Mail's Class 325s, though most of them sat unused.

Following the first carriage of mail by rail and sorting of mail in transit during the nineteenth century, only in the early twenty-first century did travelling sorters finally leave the trains. Nevertheless, although the volume now carried is considerably diminished, mail trains continue to form an important part of the United Kingdom's postal service.

Class 90/1 no. 90129 *Frachtverbindungen* ('Freight connection') heads the Warrington to Willesden mail, photographed at Warrington Bank Quay station, 6 April 2000.

# PLACES TO VISIT

*Bath Postal Museum*, 27 Northgate, Bath BA1 1AJ.
    Telephone: 01225 460333. Website: info@bathpostmuseum.org

*The British Postal Museum & Archive*, Freeling House, Phoenix Place, London WC1X 0DL.
    Telephone: 020 7239 2570.
    Website www.postalheritage.org.uk
    Public search room for archive items including Post Office records, photographs, and stamp artwork, based in central London, open throughout the week; Museum Store in Debden, Essex, containing larger items including pillar boxes and vehicles, open on selected dates throughout the year. The collection also includes one of the finest restorations of a TPO carriage to be seen, a 1908 LNWR sorting carriage, usually on display at different locations around the country. Contact BPMA for access details.

*The National Railway Museum*, Leeman Road, York YO26 6XJ. Telephone: 01926 621261. Website: www.nrm.org.uk

Fortunately, a number of mail carriages have entered the collections of various railway preservation societies. A few of these (below) also run special 'mail by rail' events, frequently also recreating the trackside mailbag-exchange operation.

*Didcot Railway Centre*, Didcot, Oxfordshire OX11 7NJ.
    Telephone: 01235 817200. Website: www.didcotrailwaycentre.org.uk

*Great Central Railway*, Great Central Station, Great Central Road, Loughborough, Leicestershire LE11 1RW.
    Telephone: 01509 230726. Website: www.gcrailway.co.uk

*Nene Valley Railway*, Wansford Station, Stibbington, Peterborough PE8 6LR.
    Telephone: 01780 784444. Website: www.nvr.org.uk

# FURTHER READING

While travelling post offices, their history and postmarks have been written about quite extensively, the far larger fleet of trains carrying just mails have received scant attention. Parcels and mail carriages and vans are often included in publications listing the rolling stock of specific railway companies. The publications below are some of the author's favoured reading:

Bayliss, D. A. *The Post Office Railway London*. Turntable Publications, 1978.

De Lacy-Spencer, R. *The Railway Letter Stamps of Great Britain and Ireland 1891–1947*. Moorside Publishing Ltd, 2000.

Ewen, H. L'Estrange. *No. 1 Priced Catalogue of the Newspaper and Parcel Stamps Issued by the Railway Companies of the United Kingdom 1855–1906*. 1906.

Goodbody, A. M. *The Railway Sub Offices of Great Britain*. The Railway Philatelic Group, 1983.

Hitches, M. *The Irish Mail*. Sutton Publishing, 2000.

Johnson, P. *An Illustrated History of the Travelling Post Office*. Oxford Publishing Co, 2009.

Pipe, W. T. *Postmarks of British and Irish Railway Stations 1840–1997*. Railway Philatelic Group, 2001.

Stanway, L. C. *Mails under London*. Association of Essex Philatelic Societies, 2000.

White, W. *A Look at the Night Mail, Travelling Post Offices – A History*, Friends of M30272M TPO Group, 2007.

Wilson, H. S. *The Travelling Post Offices of Great Britain and Ireland, Their History and Postmarks*. The Railway Philatelic Group, 1996.

# INDEX